CELEBRATING THE FAMILY NAME OF LANE

Celebrating the Family Name of Lane

Walter the Educator

Silent King Books
a WhichHead Entertainment Imprint

Disclaimer

This book is a literary work; the story is not about specific persons, locations, situations, and/or circumstances unless mentioned in a historical context. Any resemblance to real persons, locations, situations, and/or circumstances is coincidental. This book is for entertainment and informational purposes only. The author and publisher offer this information without warranties expressed or implied. No matter the grounds, neither the author nor the publisher will be accountable for any losses, injuries, or other damages caused by the reader's use of this book. The use of this book acknowledges an understanding and acceptance of this disclaimer.

Celebrating the Family Name of Lane is a memory book that belongs to the Celebrating Family Name Book Series by Walter the Educator. Collect them all and more books at WaltertheEducator.com

USE THE EXTRA SPACE TO DOCUMENT YOUR FAMILY MEMORIES THROUGHOUT THE YEARS

LANE

The name of Lane, both strong and true,

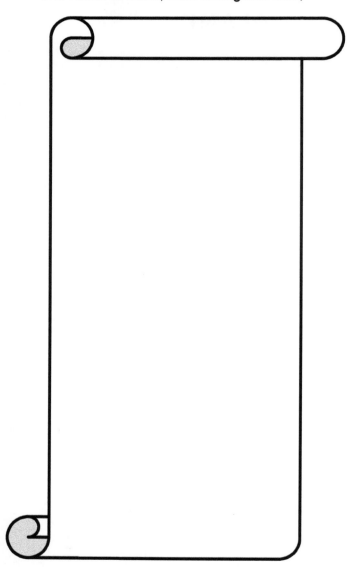

A path that's wide, a road that grew.

Through winding ways and skies so vast,

The Lane name walks, it will not pass.

With roots that stretch through earth and sky,

The Lane name stands, it will not die.

In every step, in every stride,

They move as one, with hearts full of pride.

Through fields of gold, through cities bright,

They find their way, they seek the light.

With every choice, with every dream,

The Lane name flows, a steady stream.

In laughter shared, in moments deep,

The Lane name's love is strong to keep.

In every heart, in every face,

They carry forth a boundless grace.

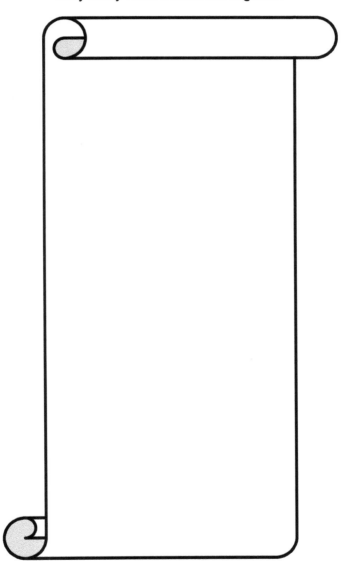

Through trials faced, through storms of night,

They rise again, they chase the light.

With courage fierce, with hearts so bold,

The Lane name shines, it will unfold.

In hands that craft, in minds that soar,

The Lane name opens every door.

Through every dream, through every goal,

They strive to reach, they seek the whole.

Through quiet moments, through the song,

The Lane name finds where they belong.

In every bond, in every tie,

The Lane name reaches to the sky.

With hearts that burn, with wills that stand,

The Lane name echoes through the land.

Through every year, through every call,

The Lane name rises above it all.

Through every path, through every lane,

The family marches, free of strain.

In all they build, in all they seek,

The Lane name thrives, forever unique.

So here's to Lane, both bright and true,

A name that holds both old and new.

With strength and love, they take their stand,

The Lane name carved upon the land.

ABOUT THE CREATOR

Walter the Educator is one of the pseudonyms for Walter Anderson. Formally educated in Chemistry, Business, and Education, he is an educator, an author, a diverse entrepreneur, and he is the son of a disabled war veteran.
"Walter the Educator" shares his time between educating and creating. He holds interests and owns several creative projects that entertain, enlighten, enhance, and educate, hoping to inspire and motivate you. Follow, find new works, and stay up to date with Walter the Educator™

at WaltertheEducator.com